THE BODHI TREE

The Bodhi Tree

Told by Greta James

Illustrated by Joanna Troughton

GEOFFREY CHAPMAN

LONDON 1971

Geoffrey Chapman Ltd
18 High Street, Wimbledon, London SW19

Geoffrey Chapman (Ireland) Ltd
5-7 Main Street, Blackrock, Co. Dublin

First published 1971

ISBN 0 225 65827 5

Printed in Great Britain by Butler & Tanner Ltd Frome and London

Contents

About this Book   9

Part One   The King's Son

1 The Prince is born   13
2 The Prince grows up   17
3 Siddartha and his Princess   22
4 The contest of the suitors   26
5 The court of happiness   31
6 The first visit of Siddartha to the city   36
7 The King's dream and the second visit of
  Siddartha to the city   40
8 Yasodhara's dream and Siddartha's departure   49

Part Two   The Time has Come

9 Siddartha begins his search   59
10 The sacrifice   65
11 The sorrows of Siddartha and the coming of joy   71
12 Siddartha finds a way through the darkness   78
13 The Buddha returns home   84
14 The Buddha teaches his people   90

For Susan, Losi, Kemi
and their brothers and sisters

"A little knowing, little have I told
Touching the Teacher and the Ways of Peace."

About this Book

About 500 B.C. there lived in the great country of India a wonderful person, who became one of the greatest teachers of the eastern peoples. Siddartha was born in a palace. His father was a great King, his mother a Queen and, when he grew up, he married a beautiful Princess. Then he decided to go away and live as a poor man. He learned how ordinary people lived. He discovered one of the greatest of secrets, the secret of real happiness, and he taught many people to understand. Even kings and priests listened to him. When he died he was not forgotten, but lived on in the hearts of those who loved goodness and gentleness. Millions of people in the world today are called "Buddhists" or followers of the Buddha, as Siddartha was later called. The Buddha means the enlightened one.

Many years ago I visited a small white building in the city of Colombo, which is in Ceylon, the island which lies to the south of India. All around the walls were paintings showing events in the life of the Prince Siddartha, but as I did not know the stories about him, I could not understand the pictures very well. So I decided to find out about the stories. They had been written down in English by Sir Edwin Arnold in a long poem called *The Light of Asia*.

Here then are some of the stories of the Buddha, who was born Prince Siddartha. He was very rich and lived in a wonderful palace set in a vast garden. He had everything in life which a man could wish for, but he found out that most of the people in his father's kingdom, those living in the city outside the palace gardens and those in the countryside outside the city, were mostly poor. They were often sick and in pain and unhappy.

He went away from his home, leaving his father, the King, leaving his beautiful young wife to bear his baby son. He gave up the kingdom, which he would have ruled after his father died. Instead he lived many years as a beggar and he became a holy man. He sat down and thought and thought and thought about the joys and sorrows of all the people in the world and wondered how they could become happier, with a deep-down inside happiness. He knew from experience that having plenty of money and plenty of beautiful things did not bring happiness.

Then one morning, as he watched the sun rising, he made a great discovery. He found the great secret of a happy life. And from that day he left the place where he had sat all alone under the Bodhi tree, and went back to teach the people. He returned to his father's kingdom. He remained a beggar and was never a prince or a king, but all who saw him and heard him thought he was greater than any prince or king. Each day he shone out among men like the sun, bringing light and understanding, warmth and love, and giving out to others the secret that he found, that a person can have everything he wants and still be unhappy, that he can have nothing at all and yet discover joy.

Part One

The King's Son

1. The Prince is Born

In that part of India which lies just to the south of the snow-capped Himalayas, the highest mountains in the world, there once lived the Sakya people ruled over by King Suddhodana and his Queen Maya.

One night Queen Maya dreamed a wonderful dream. She saw in her dream a huge and splendid elephant, white as milk and with six tusks! It seemed to her as if this great beast rushed towards her and then, by a miracle, entered into her body. When she awoke her heart was filled with joy and that morning dawned so beautiful that it was as if the flowers on the hillsides and even the waves on the sea tossed and danced with joy. Perhaps the dawn wind had told them that there would soon come to the earth a child who would be a teacher, one of those greatest of men, who can help people to understand the difficult things about life, which even grown-up people, even quite old people, cannot quite understand. At the king's court were wise men who could explain about dreams. They told the Queen that she would have a son and that he would be wonderfully wise.

So when it was time for the child to be born, Queen Maya lay in the palace garden, on a bed of flowers sheltered by a leafy bower. The newborn child was washed in a little stream, which had sprung up nearby. Later the Queen and her baby were carried back to the palace in a palanquin with four bearers holding up the poles at the four corners. And men said that the four bearers were four mighty angels, who with a host of their followers had come from heaven to celebrate the birth of the child. Angels from the south came riding on blue horses and carrying shields of sapphire; angels from the west were on blood-red horses and carried coral shields; angels from the east wore silver robes and carried shields of pearl and they rode on white horses, while angels of the north had yellow robes and yellow horses. Invisibly they all came until they reached the earth and then the four greatest angels appeared as bearers to carry the child and his mother back to the palace.

In honour of his new-born son and of the great future which the wise men had foretold for him, the King declared throughout his kingdom a great festival and holiday. The town was cleaned and decorated and the trees all hung with flags and lamps. The country people came into the towns to see the sights and to enjoy the entertainments. There were jugglers and sword players and lovely dancers with swinging dresses and bells on their feet. There were wrestlers and shows of wild beasts and there were musicians of all kinds making lovely music. Merchants came too and all the smaller cities of the land sent tribute to the King and many rich gifts in honour of his son, who would surely in time to come ascend his father's throne and rule as their king.

Then through the thronging crowds came an old grey-haired man, who people said was a saint, a very holy person of great wisdom. Even the King paid him reverence and the Queen would have laid her child at his feet to ask for his blessing, but the old man stopped her. Kneeling down, he bent his face to the ground before the child and he said that he saw on the boy's body all the holy signs of great goodness and blessing to come in the future. He told the King that his son would become famous, but that he would bring his father a great sorrow. He said also that Queen Maya would

not live to see either that sorrow or the greatness of her son.

And so it happened; for the Queen soon died. Until his eighth year the Prince was brought up by a Lady of the court.

2. *The Prince Grows Up*

When the boy, Siddartha, was eight years old, the King decided that it was time for him to have teachers, so he summoned his council and asked his counsellors: "Who is the wisest man in my kingdom? He must be the teacher for my son." And all the counsellors replied at once, "O King, Viswamitra is our wisest man!" So the King sent for Viswamitra and he came to the palace to teach the Prince.

Having heard that the boy already knew how to read and write, the wise man recited to him a verse of their sacred scriptures and asked him if he could write it down. The child smiled at his teacher and with a stick began to write the letters in the dust, and when he had written it down, he began to write it again in another language and then in another one again. These different languages did not have just different words and different sounds but the way of writing the letters was quite different too, yet the little boy seemed to know all the languages and even the old picture writing of the ancient peoples.

Then Viswamitra knew that he could teach the Prince nothing about letters and languages so he asked him to count and the boy knew all the numbers too, even the fractions and also the millions and million millions that only the gods and wisest men ever used. He knew also the measurements, that which would measure a speck of dust or the largest which would reach to heaven. Viswamitra was overcome with wonder, for the little boy already seemed to have all his knowledge, yet he was not boastful or proud and sat still modestly and reverently before the teacher. Moreover it was not only book knowledge which the Prince had, for he was very strong and very graceful; he could ride and drive a chariot with horses and compete in many games.

Not only did Siddartha have great skill of body and skill of mind, but he had also something else which set him above his fellows. He had the great gift for understanding and pity and he knew when any person or any animal was in pain. In all his life he had never himself known sorrow or pain, yet he understood how others could feel. Sometimes with the boys of the palace he rode in chariot races and he, being the most skilful of all, could always win, but if for a moment he felt his horses gasping for breath or knew that one of his friends was feeling miserable at losing, then instantly he knew that he must banish the pain and the sorrow, so he would check his horses and let his friend win.

Then came a day when the Prince really knew for the first time how cruelty and suffering could spoil the brightness and the beauty of the world. It was a lovely spring day and the palace gardens were looking their best; overhead came a flock of wild swans, going to their nesting places further inland. As they flew over they called to each other and the notes were like a love song.

The Prince had a cousin, a boy named Devadatta, who was very clever with a bow and arrow and he thought it would be fun to try to shoot one of the swans. His arrow pierced the wing of a swan which fell like a stone and lay bleeding upon the ground. It flapped wildly with its uninjured wing, snapping with its beak. The bird was hurt and angry and dangerous but Siddartha had no fear. He went close, sat on the ground and resting the great bird across his lap, he soothed it until it was quiet; then quickly he drew out the arrow. Then, because he did not really know what pain was, he took the arrow and pressed its point into his own arm, so that he could feel how it hurt and know a little more what the swan had felt.

Then came a messenger from his cousin asking for the body of the swan that he had brought down, but Siddartha replied that the swan was not dead.

"My cousin," he said, " has killed only the speed in flight of the swan. If the bird were dead, it would belong to the killer, but it is alive and because I have loved it and cared for it, it is now mine. Yet if my cousin is not satisfied, we will call the wise men and they shall judge."

So the counsellors were called and the matter was explained to them. And there stood up among them one whom no one could ever remember having seen before and he gave judgment for the Prince, saying: "He who saves a life, has a better claim than he who spoils or destroys life." All agreed with this judgment, but later when men talked of it and the King tried to find the strange priest who had spoken, he seemed to have disappeared. Someone said they had seen a snake slide through the doorway and the wise men whispered that a god had come to give judgment.

Some days later, when the swan, its wing healed, had flown away after its fellows, the King called Siddartha to him and said, "My son, this is the loveliest time of the year, when the leaves and flowers are opening and the grass is green and the land is ploughed for the sowing of the seed. Come and ride out with me and I will show you all the kingdom, which one day will be yours to rule."

So the King and the Prince rode out on fine horses through the countryside. They watched the farmers with their ploughs breaking up the rich soil and the sowers sowing seed; they saw the streams among the palm trees and the young blossoms and grasses on all the banks and in the hedges. Squirrels and lizards, bees and beetles and all living things were active and happy in the sunshine. In the woods, birds sang and built their nests. The doves cooed and the kites flew high up and the peacocks strutted on the steps of the temple. In the villages the drums were beating for weddings and all the people seemed to be gay.

Prince Siddartha was very glad when he saw these things, but he also saw other things which his father did not notice. He saw how hard the farmer, who was ploughing, had to work and how he goaded and urged on the oxen drawing the plough, so that both men and animals were straining and sweating in the heat. He saw too how many animals hunted each other. The lizard caught the ant, the snake caught the lizard and the kite killed the snake for food. Some of the birds preyed on fish or caught other birds. All life was beautiful and yet in life there was also struggle and pain. And the Prince, who had such a tender heart, knew that it was this thing about life, which men would like to understand, but they could not understand. He knew too that if he were to try and understand things, he would have to be quiet by himself and think about it often.

So Siddartha on his return sat in the palace gardens under a shady tree and time passed and it was high noon and then later it was evening. But though the sun moved across the sky the tree's shadow did not move, but stayed to shade the boy who was thinking so deeply. And the tree itself murmured in sympathy knowing that the Prince sat with a dark shadow of grief upon his heart and mind. So it was that while he was still a boy, Siddartha began to think in a way which would finally lead him to understanding, so that he could become a helper and teacher of other men.

3. Siddartha and his Princess

When a Prince comes of age it is usual for him to have a separate palace of his own, but so rich was King Suddhodana of the Sakya people, that he built three palaces for his son, when Siddartha was eighteen years old.

One palace was built of cedar wood to keep out the chill of winter days, one was of marble which would be cool in the hottest summer and the third was of brick covered with blue glazed tiles that matched the blue of the skies in spring. Each palace was surrounded with lovely gardens, with lawns and woods and streams. And in these three palaces Siddartha passed his time with much pleasure. But now and again there came to his mind the thought of all the things which could make men sad or ill and then he would become grave and silent.

This worried the King, for he hoped that his son would become a great King, a warrior and ruler of men, proud and strong and active. Pity and self-denial were not the virtues of a King. So one day King Suddhodana called together his

Ministers of State and asked their advice. What could he do to turn his son from his quiet brooding?

Then the eldest Minister said: "O mighty King, the boy is young but surely he is lonely. Let us find him companions and perhaps a beautiful wife! Then love shall fill his thoughts and the beauty of his wife will bind him to his kingdom." All the others agreed, but the King then said, "How can we be sure that those we choose for him will win his favour?"

Then one of the Ministers said, "For every man, there is always one face which seems to be the fairest, one form which is the dearest. We must find for the Prince such a bride, one whom he will love so much that it will be like an enchantment. Let us have a sports and dancing festival and bring all the girls in the Kingdom and let the Prince then give the prizes. So all the most beautiful, the most graceful and the most skilful of young women will pass in front of him and surely there will be one whom he will choose."

The King agreed and a great festival of pleasure was held. All the lovely Indian girls came, looking like flowers in their gayest and brightest clothes with jewels in their dark hair. After many games and contests, the Prince sat on a high throne above the throng of people and the prizewinners passed before him to receive their prizes. But sitting there so high above them all, he seemed far away, hardly noticing the individual girls as they walked up to him, and because there was already something so quiet about him, the girls came and passed nervously with downcast eyes.

Then last of all came the lovely Yasodhara, who was so very beautiful that no one had ever even tried to describe how beautiful she was and those who stood near the Prince saw that he suddenly looked up as she came near. She, too,

looked at him and smiled. Then the Prince rose to give her her prize, but found to his distress that all the gifts were already given and there was no prize left. At once, he took from his neck a golden chain with emeralds and he gave it to her as a girdle, himself fastening it around her waist. They looked at each other and it was as if they had known each other long ago, had known each other before and now met again. They recognized each other and they belonged together and they must always be so.

When it was reported to the King how Siddartha had changed at the sight of Yasodhara and how he had given her a special gift, he sent messengers to the girl's father to ask if she might come to the Prince as his wife. But it was the custom of the Sakya people that a man should win his bride in open contest against any other man who might desire her. Only if Prince Siddartha would compete in the games; only if he proved himself victor with the bow and arrow, also in sword play and in riding, could he win Yasodhara to be his wife. The older men shook their heads. How was the Prince, who had spent so many years living in soft luxury, quietly reading and dreaming away the time, going to excel in such trials of strength and skill?

4. *The Contest of the Suitors*

On the seventh day after the festival, when Prince Siddartha had first seen Yasodhara and loved her, all the people gathered together again to see the best young men compete for her hand in marriage. Devadatta, the Prince's cousin, was there, he who was most expert with the bow and who years before had shot down the leader swan in flight. There was Ardjuna too and he was reckoned to be the best horseman, and there was Nanda, who could wield a sword better than anyone.

Yasodhara herself came, surrounded by all her kinfolk. She rode in a litter decked with flowers and drawn by oxen, whose wide horns were tipped with gold. And lastly came Siddartha riding his great white horse, Kanaka, and he looked about him glad as always to see the thronging people, who were not usually allowed into the palace gardens. He knew that they did not live quietly and in luxury as he had always done, but worked and sweated to make a living in the fields and in the shops of the town. They seemed a little strange to him, because as a great prince he had always been kept far away from them in their busy lives, but he already wanted to know more about people. Then he saw Yasodhara and he cried aloud, "Only he who proves himself the best can be worthy of this most lovely princess. Let the contest begin and all shall see if I am too bold in claiming to be worthy of her love!"

First came the archery contest. Each suitor was given for a target a small brass drum, which he had to pierce with an arrow. Ardjuna and Nanda shot first using each a great bow of lacquered cane, bound with silver wire, and their arrows hit the mark, then Devadatta, standing even further away, shot his arrow right through the drum. The crowd shouted and cheered and the sweet Yasodhara drew her veil across her face, lest she should see the Prince fail to do as well as the others. Then Prince Siddartha took up the bow and he was so strong that as he bent it, it snapped in two. He laughed and called for a stronger bow but there did not seem to be a stronger one.

Then someone ran to the nearby temple and brought back an ancient bow so strong that none, since its owner had died, had been able even to fix the string. It was made of black steel, inlaid with gold in a wonderful design. The princes all passed it from hand to hand, admiring its beauty and the craftsmanship, but not one of them could bend the tips of the bow near enough to fix the cord. Siddartha then took it, slipped the end of the cord into its notch, so that it twanged like a harp string with a note of music and far away old and feeble folk who had been left at home heard the sound and thought it was wonderful and they were at peace. Siddartha set up his drum at a much greater distance than Devadatta had set his and he shot with the great bow, so that the arrow pierced the drum from end to end and

27

went on to disappear out of sight across the field. So Siddartha had won the first contest.

Next came the sword competition. Each man had to take a sword and, with one sweep, cut through a small tree. Devadatta had the first go this time and the branch which he cut through was as thick as six fingers together. Ardjuna's tree was even thicker and Nanda, who was champion of the sword play, managed one even thicker still. But the tree which Siddartha cut through was twice as thick as the one Nanda cut and so cleanly and swiftly did he cut through it that, for a moment or two, the tree stayed upright and everyone thought he had failed. Then the tree fell and Siddartha had won again.

In the horse racing the Prince was an easy victor, for no one could keep up with Kanaka, his swift white horse, the best in all the kingdom. The other princes complained that this was not a fair test of skill, as Siddartha could obviously afford to have the best horse. Then they brought from the palace stables a great black stallion, which had never been ridden, had never felt a saddle and had not even been shod. Most of the princes were thrown almost as soon as they mounted the black horse, but Ardjuna did well for he kept his seat while the horse reared and plunged and tried to dislodge him. Then suddenly the angry beast swung his head, caught Ardjuna's foot in his teeth and dragged him down. He would have killed him had not the grooms run in with ropes and chains to hold the animal. The people were afraid then and many begged the Prince not to risk his life on this great untamed horse, but Siddartha walked forward and quietly told the grooms to let go the ropes and set the horse free. The great black beast stood trembling and sweat-

ing, but still determined not to have a man near him, so Siddartha just went up to him, placed a hand upon his forehead and rubbed his nose and patted him on the neck and the night-black horse stood still. Finally he allowed Siddartha to get on his back and he carried him around the field. Everyone was amazed and they cried out, but still the horse was quiet under Siddartha's hands and all hailed him as the victor.

Then up came Supprabuddha, who was the father of the

lovely Princess Yasodhara, and he said: "Dear Prince, we loved you the best and desired to have you for her husband, but we could not know how in your palaces and gardens and living so much alone you could have learned such skill or developed such strength as you have shown today. You have indeed won your prize, your bride."

Yasodhara herself then came to the Prince who was still standing with his arm around the black horse's neck. Her dress was black and gold, emblem of the mighty strength of the tiger. As she walked past the other princes she covered her face with her veil, but when she came to Siddartha she dropped the veil and looked into his face. Then in the fashion of her people, she hung a great wreath of flowers around his neck as a mark of deep respect. She gave him her hand and they walked through the crowd of people as if they walked alone together.

5. The Court of Happiness

Soon Siddartha and Yasodhara were married. The wedding feast was held according to the ancient customs of the Sakya people. Wise men read the magic signs and said when the time was most favourable. Then they took a cup of milk coloured red and floated two straws in it and at once the straws came close together and floated side by side. So it was foretold that the Prince and his bride would always love each other very dearly. To celebrate the wedding the King gave gifts to the wise men and to the Temple and he gave money and food to the people so that all could celebrate the wedding. Old Supprabuddha gave his daughter to the Prince in a wonderful marriage ceremony and Siddartha was enchanted by his lovely Princess just as the King had hoped.

The King was so happy that he ordered another palace to be built for his son and daughter-in-law. He planned that it should be more beautiful than any palace ever built in his kingdom. It stood on the lower slopes of the hills well

away from the city which lay to the south. Forests and gardens divided it from the living place of other people. To the north of it rose the great peaks of the Himalaya mountains, snowclad and beautiful, and from the palace one could see on clear days the most wonderful view on earth. One could look across the plain to the thick jungles and above the jungles were the dark forests with leaping waterfalls and above these again were the eternal snows of the mighty mountain peaks, range upon range leading the eye upward and upward. Often as one looked across the great space of the earth, mists would hide the lower land and the white mountain peaks appeared far off as if high in the blue heaven.

The palace itself was built with terraces and arches and cloisters all carefully carved with pictures and symbols of the gods and with good luck signs. The inner gates were of white marble, pink-veined, with marble steps and jewelled arches. Then there were sandalwood doors richly carved and, further in, tall columns, fountains, courtyards and pavilions and fish-pools with gold and coloured fish. There were rose gardens, and doves nesting in the trees and stately peacocks strutted in the courtyards. Brilliantly coloured parrots and other bright birds swung and flew among all the trees and flowers. Monkeys ran in and out and were tame and the squirrels also came to be fed.

Most beautiful of all were all the girls and attendants that the King chose to wait upon the Prince and his bride. Every one of them was young and lovely, quick and graceful and obedient. The Prince and Princess had all they could want, anything they asked for was brought at once; anything they wanted done, was done.

In the innermost court of the palace was the special room for Yasodhara. It had as an entrance a courtyard open to the sky and in the middle of this was a wonderful white marble fountain inlaid with pink agate. The court was cool and quiet. Beyond this was the inner chamber hung with golden silk and lighted night and day with perfumed lamps, which always gave the same soft golden light.

At any moment, if it was desired, sweet music would sound and the most delicious food and ice-cool drinks would be served. Only the most beautiful of all the chosen attendants were allowed within the inner court. Some were musicians and there were dancers and some who served the food and drink and some who just stood and fanned the Prince and Princess so that no feeling of heat or tiredness should come to them. The sweetest spices scented the air and everything was as lovely as one could possibly imagine or devise. So here lived Siddartha in the greatest luxury and in all the happiness of his love for Yasodhara. He slept and ate and talked and listened to music. Everything seemed quite perfect.

It was, indeed, the King's command that nothing should break upon the peace and happiness of his son. No one was to mention death or old age and there was to be no hint at all of any sorrow or pain or sickness. Any attendant who felt at all faint or ill had to leave at once. Even of tiredness there must be no sign. If a tiny white hair appeared in the dark tresses of a dancing girl, she was banished at once. At night attendants went carefully through all the courts and gardens removing every dead flower, every dead leaf. In this way the King hoped that he could keep from his son all sad thoughts.

Not content with this, King Suddhodana had a great wall built round the palace and put in massive gates of brass, which were difficult to open. It took a hundred men to roll back the doors and the sound of it could be heard many miles away. Inside these great outer gates were built other gates, and inside this a third set. Only through these triple gates, all guarded, could anyone enter or leave. The guards at the gates had strict instructions that they should let pass in or out only those who had the King's leave. It was not even given to the Prince himself to say who could come or go from his palace. So in the height of luxury and splendour

Siddartha and Yasodhara lived, but the Prince was really a prisoner, like a bird in a cage of gold.

Though he was so shut away in his palace, far from any sight or sound of the outside world, with nothing at all to remind him of any sadness, the Prince could not forget what he had once glimpsed in the world of men. Sometimes terrible visions came to him in dreams and he would wake up in the night feeling afraid. Sometimes the wind blew through the palace windows and whispered to the Prince that it came from far away.

One day he set upon a window-sill a stringed instrument and the winds blowing across the strings made music, but it was like a sad song which said: "O Prince you rest here in your palace, but we do not rest. Like man, we do not know where we come from or whither we go, but we must wander over the world and we see much to make for sadness. All your pleasures here are like the music we make upon these strings, but the music will not satisfy you for ever. The world is waiting, Siddartha, and it is waiting for you. Men in the world could be happier because of you. Do not sleep much longer Siddartha. People are waiting. Many of them are sad and sick and the world is often a cruel place. Don't you remember, Siddartha? We are waiting for you. Do come!"

And Siddartha stayed with his bride and did not seem to hear.

6. The First Visit of Siddartha to the City

One evening, as the Prince Siddartha sat with his wife Yasodhara in the midst of their attendants, Chitra, most beautiful of the storytellers, came to entertain them. She told wonderful tales of ancient times and of far distant places and she also spoke of lands in the far west, where the people had pale skins and where, at night, the sun sank into the great sea. Chitra's musical voice seemed to Siddartha like an echo of the wind's song and as his thoughts went out to the distant lands and to the far peoples, he longed to be able to spread wings and fly like a bird across the mountains and seas and to see the whole earth.

Then suddenly he knew that the many gates and especially the great brass gates of his palace were shutting him in, shutting him away from the great world of ordinary people living and working hard, being happy and often unhappy. And once this thought had come to him, Siddartha was restless and even Yasodhara could not reassure him or make him quite forget the world outside his palace.

Next day he ordered that his chariot and horses should be brought and, when it was reported to the King, the King's messengers ran throughout all the great city of Kapilavastu and ordered that all the blind and the maimed, cripples and the sick, the old and the lepers were all to stay hidden for the whole day. Streets were specially cleaned, houses were made tidy and decorated and the holy places re-decorated. Criers went out through all the streets in the early morning calling out the King's orders, so that only the people who were young and healthy and the little children gathered together, dressed in their best, to see the Prince ride by.

At noon he came, riding in a gaily painted chariot drawn by two strong and slow white oxen. The people shouted greetings and Siddartha was glad to see their happiness. Yet he wondered that they could be so happy, when they had so much less than he had. But as he passed through the gay crowds of cheering people, there came forward, unmindful of the King's orders, a very old man. He was very poor and lived in a very poor hut. He was shrivelled up and almost blind and he shook with weakness and also with fright, because of the loud noises and the crowding of the people. Hardly able to stand his ground, he stood clutching tight on a stick and holding out his hand to beg for bread. Some people tried to hide him, but it was too late. The Prince had noticed the old man.

In all his life, except for the one previous visit to his kingdom, Siddartha had lived only with the most beautiful things and with young and beautiful people. For many months since his marriage he had lived among great riches and things of such rare beauty that all this had become for him commonplace. Where other people would have gasped

37

with wonder and delight, Siddartha would not have noticed anything at all for he had become so used to everything being only of the best. But to him old age and poverty and the ugliness of a man were new, surprising, terrible things. Turning to Channa, his charioteer, he asked:

"Whatever is this dreadful being? Are men sometimes made like this? Why does he look so terribly thin? What does he mean when he begs for food lest he should die?"

And Channa, who was just a sensible, ordinary and practical man, had to explain these things to him as one might explain things to a child for the first time.

"Sweet Prince," he replied, "this is just an ordinary man, who has lived for a very long time. Once he was strong and stood straight and had bright eyes, but now he is like a lamp when the oil burns low. Soon his life will flicker and go out."

Then the Prince asked: "Is this an unusual thing, Channa, or does it come to other men?" And Channa told him that all men became old if they lived for long. But still the Prince could not quite understand. "Shall I, too, grow old?" he asked.

And then a frightening thought seized him. Yasodhara, his lovely young wife. Could she, too, grow old and ugly and lose her beauty and grace and strength? Would those who served them also grow old? And when Channa told him that this would be so, the Prince turned away, sad at heart and asked to be driven home.

That evening, sitting in the court, with good food before him, soft music sounding and beautiful dancing girls stepping out to entertain him, Prince Siddartha sat silent, his eyes dark with grief. Even Yasodhara could say nothing to comfort him and when she wept, he could not find words to comfort her. Night came and killed the bright day and Siddartha looked at his attendants and looked at Yasodhara and thought only that they too would fade and die. So in this darkness his thought stopped and the next bright day beyond the darkness he could not see. All night he sat, brooding, haunted by black thoughts and no one could cheer him, no one could even make him look up.

7. *The King's Dream and the Second Visit of Siddartha to the City*

On the same night that the Prince returned from the city of Kapilavastu so shocked and saddened by his first sight of painful old age, on that night when he sat alone with his thoughts, the King his father slept and dreamed fearful dreams.

In his dream he first thought that he saw the flag of his beloved country suddenly torn down and ripped into pieces by a great wind, then flung into the dust, and there came a great host of weird grey ghosts to pick up the torn stained rags and they carried them out of the city towards the east. Then in another dream there came ten mighty elephants with silver tusks and thundering feet and they went out of the city towards the south. Siddartha the Prince was riding on the first elephant and others followed him mounted on the rest. Then in a third dream Siddartha again appeared, this time riding in a car, which shone with a great light, and it was drawn by four fiery, smoking horses, whose light with its billowing smoke was blinding. This suddenly changed into an enormous wheel, gold at the centre and with jewelled spokes and as the huge wheel turned the King saw flaming letters inscribed upon the rim. In the fifth dream again Siddartha appeared, this time beating on a great drum with an iron mace and the sound pealed through all the surrounding hills like thunder

Then there grew up before the King's eyes a tall tower. It rose and rose until it overtopped the city and there on top of the tower was Siddartha, his head crowned with clouds and from his hands came a shower of jewels falling upon the ground, so that it was raining rubies and other precious stones and all the people came running to catch the treasure as it fell. Then came the seventh and last of the King's dreams. He saw six men, and these walked past weeping and crying out, covering their mouths with their hands and showing every sign of most bitter sorrow. And with each of these seven dreams there came upon the King a terrible fear.

In the morning he sent for those who professed to interpret dreams and to explain their meaning, but not one of his wise men could tell him what these particular dreams could mean or whether they had any meaning one after the other. But suddenly there came to the gate of the King's palace an old man, who was clothed in skins and looked like a hermit or holy man. He called out to the men at the gate that they must let him in, for he wished to see the King as he had something important to say to him. The King was told and soon, because the old man had said he could explain the King's dreams, he was brought in. Then the King told the old man all his dreams and the old man bent low before him.

"O mighty King," he said, "from this house will come one who will be greater and more splendid than the sun. These should not be fearful messages for you but a great joy. The flag which you saw torn down and carried away, signifies that old beliefs will be taken away to make room for something new. The ten elephants are the ten great gifts of wisdom and the Prince shall leave your kingdom to ride on the thunder of truth across the world. The four flaming horses are the four Virtues, which shall bring your son safely through all darkness and doubt to joy and light. The wheel is the wheel of the law which he shall show to the world. The thundering drum is his speaking of the holy Word. The growing tower is like his teaching and the jewels are the treasures of goodness which shall be given to all people. Lastly the six weeping men represent the teachers of past times, for they by the new teachings shall be convinced of their foolishness."

"Rejoice, O King!" continued the old man. "Your son's inheritance is greater than your kingdom, greater than all the wealth that you can pass on to him." Then he added, "These things shall begin to come to pass in seven days and nights from now."

Then the old man turned away and the King, recovering from his surprise, sent his servants after to give him some payment, but the servants could not find him, though they looked into the Temple where men said he had gone to pray. Only in the darkness of the Temple a grey owl fluttered.

The King was not pleased by the old man's message. He could not really understand what it meant, but thought only that he would soon lose his son. He ordered the guard at the brazen gate of the Prince's palace to be doubled and he ordered more pleasures for the Prince.

Then Siddartha sent word to his father asking for his permission to ride out into the city and to see the people and he asked especially if he could go among them without any warning, so that he might see something of the ordinary daily life and not have everyone out in their best clothes and the streets full of flags to welcome him. Even now it is not so easy for the son of a king, who will himself be king in his turn, to see the people as they go about their usual work. People like to have a holiday and to put out flags, the streets are cleaned and decorated, the prince rides with an escort and all the important people come out to greet him and there are speeches. The King must have been worried by his son's request but after some thought he decided he must let the Prince go. It would not do if his son felt that he was a prisoner never allowed to come and go freely. Also, thought the King, perhaps if his son saw the ordinary life going on he would not be so distressed as he evidently had been by the sight of just one old man breaking into the picture of gaiety and happiness.

So next day, Siddartha and his servant Channa went out of the palace dressed as merchants and they wandered nearly all day in the city streets.

In the city of Kapilavastu at that time there were many craftsmen making useful and beautiful things and many merchants and traders came to the city from other places to exchange goods and farmers brought food in from the countryside. Shopkeepers sat cross-legged in front of their shops and buyers came and bargained for goods. Huge carts with enormous wheels, sometimes made of stone, passed slowly along the narrow streets. Richer people rode in litters carried at each corner by strong bearers and these sang as they went along. Women were going to and fro, for

they all had to fetch water from the well or from fountains. They carried their babies on one hip and the water jars upon their heads. There was a mill grinding meal from the corn and there was a sweet shop, swarming with flies. Dogs, often half wild, hunted in the gutters for scraps of food or snatched what they could.

The blacksmith and the armourer worked at their forges making a tremendous clanging noise as they beat on the hot iron and the brass workers made an even greater noise beating on the great brass jars with little hammers. In the school, children sat around the teacher and sang songs or chanted out their lessons for they had to learn everything from memory. In one area the people who washed cloth and those who dyed it in bright colours spread out the bright strips of cloth to dry in the sun. Priests and soldiers went this way and that and sometimes a whole street was blocked with a chain of camels coming in with their drivers from distant places. Near one market the crowds had gathered to watch a snake charmer, who droned on a pipe while from the basket in front of him, a great hooded cobra rose and swayed with the music. And then through the crowd came a wedding procession in bright painted wagons, with men walking alongside beating on their drums. Everywhere there was great bustle and activity, a lot of noise and plenty of gaiety and bright colour.

Siddartha and Channa walked among the crowds right through the city until they came to the far side. There they heard a voice calling for help. They turned aside at once and there found a poor man, who had been suddenly struck down with the plague. He was sick and helpless and half mad with despair for no one was likely to help him for fear of the disease. With no thought for himself the Prince ran to him

and he lifted the man's head upon his knee and soothed
him, as once before he had soothed the wounded swan. But
Siddartha had so little knowledge of the dreadful things that
could happen that he did not really know what was the matter.

"What is it, Channa," he asked. "Why is he crying so and
gasping for breath?" And Channa tried to explain. This
was, he said, a sort of very sudden illness which was called
"the plague". Sometimes men did not live long lives before
they grew old, for some illnesses could just appear and come
to a person and quickly take away his strength and give
him pain and even death, and when the plague had left one
person dead it usually passed on to take hold of another.
Channa begged the Prince to go away and leave the man,
for he was running risk of the terrible infection himself. But
Siddartha did not move. He went on asking Channa
questions and Channa had to tell him that illness and sickness took many different forms and that it often seemed to
come silently and unseen, like a murderer lurking in an
ambush, choosing some victims but leaving others and no
one in all the world knew at any time when he might be
taken with pain.

The Prince asked, "But Channa, do not all men then live
all the time in fear of their lives?" Channa said that men,
while they were well and happy, did not think about it but
that no one ever really knew that he would stay well and
happy for very long. There were some pains and troubles
which did not kill, but each illness affected the body and
the mind of a man and it was because of this that in time
they became old. "What happens then, Channa?" said the
Prince. "What happens when the pain is past bearing and
old age gets even older?"

"Death comes then, my Prince," replied his charioteer.
"Only a few men live to be very, very old. Most people get

sick and die before they grow old and feeble like the man you saw on your last visit. In time, all men must die." And then from nearby there came a funeral procession. "Look, dear Prince," he said, "here comes one who has died." The people passed by, carrying on a bier a man who had died and they took his body down towards the river and placed it on the appointed place. Then they lit a great fire all around him, as was the custom in that country, so that soon all that was left was a heap of ashes and these were thrown into the river to be carried away.

Prince Siddartha was shocked and quiet for in all his young and happy life he had never been allowed to see anything like this. "Is this the end for all who live?" he asked, and the kindly charioteer, who loved his master, answered him quite plainly. "Yes, all who live, all who laugh and eat and drink and love, must in the end meet with death. Some tiny thing may kill them and when they are dead, they cannot hear or see or taste or smell; they feel nothing at all. They can be burned or their bodies buried in the ground. Yet it is said that though the body dies, somehow, somewhere, life begins again, but no one in all the world has ever quite understood how this can be."

As Channa spoke, Siddartha knew that sorrow and pain and death made a mockery of the pleasure and love, which one had when one was young. Many other men had wondered and thought about this but Siddartha in that moment felt in his own heart the innermost ache in the heart of all men and knew that there must be some comfort from all dreadful thought. Men believed in God, all-powerful, ruler of the world, who had created all things and governed all things. Why did he allow men to suffer? Deep in thought, the Prince went back to his palace, Channa with him to help and guard him. In time the King heard what had happened and he was even more worried. He added yet more guards at the great brass gates and said that the gates were to be opened for no one, until after the full seven days of the prophecy had passed.

8. Yasodhara's Dream and Siddartha's Departure

The seventh day after King Suddhodana's dream passed by like other days and no danger yet had come to his son, whom he so feared he would lose. It was beautiful weather! The air was scented with flowers and the skies were clear and jewelled with stars and over the eastern peaks of the high mountains there rose at sunset a full moon. The earth seemed very still. In the day time there was the chirping of the crickets and at night occasionally a jackal yelped in the darkness or a warder called down from a palace tower. And night fell after the seventh day! Within the Prince's palace his attendants slept and almost it seemed as if a spell had been laid on all of them for they sat and lay in the great antechamber as if sleep had come upon them quite suddenly, even while they were still working or playing or sitting talking to each other. How beautiful they looked as they lay there, their dark hair and lovely faces in the soft light of silver lamps and over all a sweet perfume. One girl had roses in her hands, which she had been arranging, and another had beads which she had been threading. A third sat with a musical instrument still in her hands and her fingers were still upon the strings, while yet another lay sleeping with her arms around the baby faun-deer which she had been fondling and feeding.

In the inner room beyond great blue and crimson hangings, richly embroidered with gold, was the bedroom where Yasodhara's bed was draped in cloth of silver. The walls around were covered with pearl shell and the roof of the bed chamber was of white alabaster, richly carved and decorated. Amid all this beauty Yasodhara sat, her face in her hands, and she wept uncomforted. The Prince lay sleeping and when she turned and kissed him tenderly, he woke and begged to know what it was that frightened and distressed her.

"Darling prince," she said, "tonight I fell asleep feeling so very happy, for the child that I am soon to bear for you was fluttering against my heart. But I had a dream and I am afraid. First there came before me a great white bull with branching horns and a jewel glittered on his forehead. He went then towards the gates of the city and as he went a voice called out, 'If you cannot hold him, the glory of the city will go with him.' I went after and put my arms about his neck but I could not hold him and he burst out through the gates and went away. Then I slept but dreamed again and saw four shining angels and a great shining host from heaven sweeping down upon our city and as they came the golden flag which flies at the gate fell down and another one more glorious was raised up in its stead. Then it was dawn and a light wind came and as it fluttered the folds of the flag all could see written upon it some wondrous words and as the sun rose there fell around blossoms of a kind and of a colour we have not seen before."

The Prince tried hard to comfort his wife, saying, "Why are you sad and afraid, Yasodhara. These were beautiful dreams with lovely, good things and nothing need have frightened you." "Ah, my lord," she replied, "but the dream ended with a voice, which cried out, 'The time has come!' and then when I looked for you I could not find you for you had gone. Your pillow and your robe were here unpressed and unused and, as I rose in fear, my girdle of pearls turned suddenly into a stinging snake. All my jewels fell away from me and the flowers in my hair withered. Our bed sank into the ground and its hangings were torn and soiled. Far off I could hear the lowing of the white bull as he went far away; I could hear the bright new flag flapping on its pole and the voice was still crying, 'The time has come; the time has come!'"

"My dearest wife," said the Prince, "indeed your dreams are prophecies. The world is waiting for help, but whatever may happen, you must remember that between us there is unchanging love. I long to help men in the world, but mostly I long to help you. I must seek for something which will help others, but all the time I shall be seeking to help you." So at last Yasodhara was comforted and she slept and yet even as she fell asleep she murmured, "The time has come!"

And Siddartha, now fully awake, looked at her sleeping and looked out at the night and at the moon and stars and knew that the great moment of his choice had come. He could stay with his lovely wife, stay in his kingdom and in time rule as King, or he could go away; and then he would wander for a long time, alone and friendless in the wider world, not quite knowing yet why he had gone or for what he was seeking. Outside and inside the palace all was still;

even the wind had ceased. The whole earth and the gods in heaven were waiting for Siddartha to make his decision.

But for Siddartha there was not really any choice. Hard as it is for us to understand, he knew that the only thing he could do was to fulfil Yasodhara's dream-prophecy and go away and leave her. Everything that had ever happened to him in his life had led to this moment. The greatness of a King, the name of great battles written in blood, these were not for him. He must seek his own way, even choosing the life of an outcast. He would walk in loneliness, clad in the poorest of garments, and make a home somewhere in the jungle or find a cave, but it was essential that he should go away alone and find some secret which would heal the pain of men. Priests the people had already and many who would for payment chant the holy songs and perform the sacrifices, but nothing that was done helped men to escape illness and pain, old age and death, and though each new birth and each new generation seemed to bring new hope, to everyone the same pain and sorrow and death came at last.

The secret that I must find, thought Siddartha, must be one which will explain life in all its forms, the lower and the higher and what plants and animals and men all mean to each other living on the earth together in the same places and at the same time. There were many things which men had indeed learned since the early days, how to make fire and how to speak and then how to put down letters and words so that speech could be written down and messages sent and books written so that a man could in one age gather the wisdom of ages long gone by. And men had learned to cultivate the fields and grow crops and keep certain animals. All such discoveries had come to men after much thinking and searching and struggle and sacrifice and often even the best new things had been rejected just because they were new. Men had yet to win freedom from their own fears, their ignorance and their cruelty to each other.

What of the sacrifice that Siddartha had to make if he was to give up the rest of his life to seek to help other men? He was rich, he had everything that a man could desire to have; if he stayed in his kingdom he would stay with his beloved wife and have more children. He would rule as a great king and could do a great deal of good. He was still young and the world offered many things. He himself had never known pain or grief and had indeed lacked for nothing, but all this he must give up because nothing was so important as that he should find somewhere, something, which would show him how pain and grief, however it came to men, might be healed and how life might yet be full of joy, come what may.

Siddartha had indeed made up his mind and knew what he must do, but his heart ached for his father who would be so distressed and disappointed at his going, never understanding, and he sorrowed for his lovely wife, who must soon bear their child alone and without him and thinking he had left her. Yet he knew that his father and his wife were both part of mankind and it was for all mankind that he must go on this search. Mercifully Yasodhara slept now, the tears still not dried upon her cheeks. Silently he said farewell to her and went out through the court, where all the others were sleeping. In the ancient books it says that as he went even the earth trembled and the skies were full of faint music, for all the angelic host had come to watch his going.

Outside, Siddartha found Channa where he slept, woke him and asked for his horse Kanaka. Channa wondered how it could be that the wise man had foretold for his master such glory and power and dominion and yet here he was proposing to ride away out of his kingdom. But, as an

obedient servant he did what Siddartha asked, and fetched
the great white horse from the stables. He bridled him in
silver and put on a saddle with jewelled girth. The stirrups
were of gold and over all was a draped net of silk sewn with
seed pearls. Everyone would know that the man riding
such a beautiful horse so richly equipped must be a great
prince. As Channa brought Kanaka out to his prince the
horse neighed loudly with joy and men said later that the

angels must have spread their wings, so that those who slept heard nothing and were not disturbed.

Siddartha fondled his horse for a few moments, talking quietly to him and telling him of the long, long ride ahead; then he leaped into the saddle, but from the bit and the bridle chain no rattle came and as he rode to the gates Kanaka's feet made no sound, for it was as if silken cloth and flowers had been laid about his feet. The great brass doors in all their threefold strength, so heavy and so difficult to move, opened for the Prince to pass through and all the guards lay sleeping. No one stirred.

So all through the long night Siddartha, with Channa beside him, rode away from his kingdom and, when at last the sun rose over the eastern mountains and it was light, the Prince stayed his horse and dismounted. Quietly he said farewell to the horse Kanaka and across the saddle he laid his fine outer robes; he gave the bridle to Channa and told him to go back slowly, resting the horses on the way, and he gave Channa a last message for his father the King. Channa did as the Prince told him. He turned the horses around and set out on the return journey riding slowly, to save the tired animals and also because he dreaded the moment when he must return with the message that the great Prince had left his country.

Siddartha watched them go and then he turned again and went on alone and on foot. He was outside his own country and he knew nothing of any dangers which might await him. He only knew that he must make a journey and that he must find something which would be as a blessing to all mankind.

Part Two

The Time has Come

9. Siddartha Begins his Search

Far from the land of the Sakya people, the country of King Suddhodana, lay the kingdom of Bimbisara. It lay to the north towards the foot of the mountains and was a forested country set between five great peaks. The easternmost mountain was Ratnagiri, the hill of gems, and high up on the shoulder of this mountain was a cave reached by a narrow winding path. In this cave Siddartha made his first home after he left his palace.

In all his life he had never known any discomfort. He had had palaces for the heat of summer and the cool of the winter and he had always had attendants to bring him everything he could want. Now he lived alone in a bare cave with only a wild vine for shelter near its entrance and there he stayed through many hot days and cold nights. Mostly he sat deep in thought simply seeking in the loneliness and in the silence to try to understand about heaven and earth, about the gods and the making of the earth and of men, wondering always why it was that in this world men had to

live so short a time and then die and why it was that during
their lives they found so little happiness.

Mostly he sat so deep in thought that he did not notice
the dark shadow of the night roll over the land nor did he
hear the distant sounds of the little town or the growls of
the wild beasts in the jungle nearby. But generally the first
light of the dawn would find him standing, where he could
best see the sun rise up from the east, where he could best
hear the dawn wind as it always rippled across the fields
just before the coming of the sun. Then he would wash himself in a nearby stream and he would make his way down
the winding path into the little town and there he would
beg for bread as other holy men did in that land. He wore
a yellow robe as was the usual dress for holy men and
already his face was so sweetly radiant with love that those
who were busy all day, working to get enough to live on,
knew that they must manage to spare a little to put in his
bowl, but usually it was only the barest scraps of food and
sometimes people would just give him what they would
have thrown away.

Siddartha found many other men, most of whom begged
in the streets by day, living in other caves and places in the
hills. They too had sought to be alone to pray to God and
some also hoped to be able to help their fellow men, so
Siddartha often spoke to them and from many he learned
of ancient religions and of wise things said in the past. But
some of these men were particularly pitiful, for they had
persuaded themselves that if they could personally learn to
bear great pain without minding it at all, without perhaps
even feeling it, then they would become as the angels in
heaven, all wise and all powerful. So they tortured their own
bodies and lived half-starved, dirty and wretched, and they
really believed that in this way they were doing some good

or learning something important. Siddartha looked at them and then he looked around at the trees and the birds and he looked across the countryside and he saw many happy people in bright clothes and he could not think that it was right that men should deliberately make their lives ugly and painful and wretched.

It seemed to him that men's lives were like the drops of rain, which fall on the earth and the waters are gathered into a brook and many small streams into a river, which after many wanderings reaches the sea. But this was not the end, for over the wide rivers and lakes and over the sea, the sun shone and the warm air gathered up many little drops of moisture into the sky and soon these made the clouds and the rains fell again on the earth. It was a complete circle and round and round it went many times over. So Siddartha said to himself: "Could men's lives be like that? Do they live and then die and then return to live again and so on through many ages? Do they suffer or have joy according to some earlier experiences? Are their bad actions punished not in hell, but again here on earth and are their good actions rewarded by something better later on?"

Near the fig-grove by the mouth of Siddartha's cave there lived a family, where the young wife had one little boy whom she loved most dearly. One day the child wandered away from home and did not come when his mother called, and she could not find him, but at last after much searching she found him lying on a heap of leaves and a small snake had twined itself around his wrist. He had been playing with the snake not knowing there was any danger. Soon after he became pale and lay still and would not eat. The woman ran to her friends and neighbours but they shook their heads sadly, for they could see the mark where the snake had bitten the child. He would surely die, they said, but the mother refused to believe that her child could die from such a tiny wound. Why indeed should anything evil hurt her little boy, who had only played so innocently and with such joy in his short life? Then, as she went on and on, they suggested that the holy man who lived in the cave on the hill above her hut might be able to help her, so she carried the child up to the cave not realizing that he was already dead.

Siddartha had, long ago, taken into his arms a wounded and almost dying swan and he had healed the lovely bird and set it free once more to fly, but when the child was in his arms, he knew that he had no cure for death and that he could do nothing to bring the child back to life. Yet something had to be done to comfort the poor mother, who was quite crazed with her grief and who still felt sure he had only to say some magic word and the child would be restored to her laughing and hungry as before.

Quietly he said, "There is one thing you can try to get to help your child. You must try to find a seed of the black mustard, but you must get it from a house in which no one has ever died."

The woman then set out to go through all the village and she walked many miles through the countryside to many smaller villages trying and trying to get a seed of black mustard from a house where no one had died. But all the people there had lived in the place for a long time and their fathers and grandfathers before them. From every house they hurried out to help her, bringing seeds of the black mustard, but when she asked her question they would say:

"Oh yes, quite recently our father died."

"We had a servant who died not long ago."

"The man who sowed this seed died before the harvest."

And so it went. In every house there was some loss. Then at last the mother returned to Siddartha saying, "Death has entered every house and indeed I know now that my baby, too, is dead."

And Siddartha said, most gently, "Yes, your child is dead and nothing can be done and yours is a bitter sorrow, yet, as you have found, it is a sorrow which everyone can share with you, for in all the sweetness of life and the beauty of life there is death. This seems to be the curse for all men and this I am seeking to understand. Gladly would I give a year of my life, if that would bring your child back to life."

Siddartha had learned once more how greatly people needed comfort in deep unhappiness and how helpless anyone else was, when it came to giving comfort in such sorrow. More than ever he desired to find the secret of man's life and death.

10. The Sacrifice

One bright day, the winding path over the mountain was full
of dust and noise, as hundreds of sheep and goats were
being driven towards the town. The sheep were black and
woolly with their tails hanging down and the goats were
purest white with little perky tails sticking up, but black
and white altogether they trotted along trying to stop and
snatch some grass or nibble a few leaves as they went, and
the shepherd hurried them on, so that they went on bleat-
ing and crying. When an animal wandered off on the hill-
side, the shepherd flung a stone with his sling and so brought
it back on to the road.

Siddartha, who was on his daily journey into the little
town, stood and watched them going by and then he noticed
a ewe in great distress. She had twin lambs and while one
was skipping along ahead of her the other had been hurt
and was limping far behind. Anxiously she ran backwards
and forwards between them, afraid that one might be lost
and each time that she tried to go back to the injured lamb

the shepherd shouted and threw his stones to frighten her and the rest of the flock pushed on against her. As soon as Siddartha saw what the trouble was, he went forward and picked up the little hurt lamb and carried it upon his shoulders and the ewe knew that her lamb was safe and ran at his side keeping her eye on the other one that ran and skipped so well ahead.

Then Siddartha said to himself: "It is better to do even

one thing, which will relieve even an animal of pain and fear, than to sit in grief and in prayer for all the pain and fear in the world."

So Siddartha walked that day amid the flock of sheep and goats and soon he spoke to the herdsman and asked him why he was travelling with this great flock towards the town, for by now the sun was high in the sky and the heat was great. The herdsman said that the great King Bimbisara was holding a great service of prayer to the gods and he would be offering a sacrifice of at least a hundred sheep and a hundred goats and all of these had to be the most perfect animals that could be found in his kingdom. The Prince and the herdsman went on slowly with the animals and it was near evening when they came to the city which lay some way beyond the little town that the Prince visited each day.

They passed through the city streets and the people busy in the markets and in the workshops drew on one side to watch them go by. The blacksmith stopped a moment with his hammer lifted up and the iron on the anvil went cold; the weaver stopped his loom for a moment and the scribe sat with his pen in his hand, while his customer waited for him to write. The money changer suddenly lost count of his coins and his strings of shells, which were used for small change, and while a shopkeeper left his shop to stare, a white bull fed hungrily from one of the bins of corn. The women too came to their doors to watch the herdsman and the beasts go by and all saw the Prince walking in his beggar's robes looking more royal and more noble than ever, walking like a king, and they saw that his face was kind.

The people whispered together and ran telling each other that a great and holy man from the hills had come. And Siddartha looked about him in the city and saw the people running to and fro and thought that they too looked like the sheep and goats being driven along and hustled and worried by many things, until they too would come to their deaths in time. The coming of a holy man was reported to the King, who was in the temple surrounded by many white-robed priests. Upon a great altar burned a fire of scented logs and this was being fed with oil and spices and wine. This was called the lesser sacrifice, but it was also done to cover the burning smell which came up from the greater sacrifice, as one by one animals were being killed to make an offering for the god.

This was the custom of the country and it was a part of their religion. For many thousands of years men had supposed that the gods, who ruled the world, who had made man in the beginning and who had control of life and death and could send or take away pain and disease and decide whether the harvest would be good or bad, were like great kings who had to be made happy with gifts and food, so all that was best in the land was laid upon the altar and burned to make a sacrifice. In the olden times, men had killed other men, especially when they went to war and got prisoners, and even some people had brought their own children for sacrifice, until at last a great Teacher had come to show them that each human life was important; but when human sacrifice was no longer carried out, animal sacrifice was carried out instead. Men were still convinced that such sacrifice was necessary if the next year's harvest was to be good, if the King and his people were to be well and happy, if they were to win any wars against other people and so on. They never really thought then that in time the King would die and in time all the people then alive would die, for children were born every day and life seemed to go on just the same and hardly anyone really thought of trouble or pain until it came to him.

All around the great altar was a sort of gutter which widened out in front like a pond and the gutter all around the altar and the pond was full of blood from the animals that were being sacrificed. And all the people believed that the gods would be pleased. As Siddartha reached the door of the temple, a priest was standing at the altar holding his knife to the throat of a horned goat. He called out that he would place upon the goat all the King's wrong deeds and he called upon the gods to accept the sacrifice. And as the blood flowed and the animal was killed, and as the great fire then burned up the flesh, so it was thought that any evil which may have been done would be burned away and the King saved from any punishment or any kind of ill. And if the King was well and strong, then his whole country would be well and strong too.

Siddartha stood inside the temple doors; he saw the sacrifice and the blood and smelt the awful smell of burning flesh which could not be hidden by all the perfumes and scented woods. He looked at the King, who was happy that animals should die so that he might feel free from any sin. But suddenly it was as if the whole temple was filled by the presence of Siddartha. No one attempted to stop him as he stepped forward, forbade the priest to strike the next terrified goat now being dragged to the altar and then set the animal free.

Everyone was still, for in that land everyone, even a king, must respect a holy man and Siddartha turned to the King and said:

"How can you sit here praying for mercy from the gods when you, who are as a god to these poor beasts, show them no mercy?"

Then he went on to speak of the beauty of the world and of life in the world and of the great evil of causing pain and taking life. For some time he spoke and as they listened even the priests hid their blood-stained hands under their robes and the high priest threw away his knife and the fire upon the altar went out. The King listened also and was quiet and went back to his palace. The next day he sent out a proclamation throughout the land, that henceforth no animal was to be slain not even for sacrifice and not even for food, for in this land there was plenty of grain and beautiful fruit and the people did not need to kill animals for food. And so it was always after that, that Siddartha taught that it was not right for man to give any pain to animals or to take any pleasure or any profit from the killing of animals.

King Bimbisara asked Siddartha to come again to him and as he learned more from him, he begged him to stay in his capital city and become the teacher of his people. He offered Siddartha a palace and beautiful rooms, even a lovely woman to be with him and many attendants, but the Prince who had already given up his own palace and the wife he loved could not be tempted to stay. He had learned much and he was already convinced that the worst thing anyone could do was to increase, by anything he did, the pain and grief of other living beings, but he had not yet found the truth that he was seeking and he did not think that he would find it in Bimbisara's kingdom or indeed even in the mountain cave which he had left. So after six years in that land, Siddartha set out again on his wanderings.

11. The Sorrows of Siddartha and the Coming of Joy

In the far north-west of India, in the riverside forests not far from the thorny wastes and sandhills of a great desert, was the little village of Senani. Here in the woods Siddartha sought for refuge, still seeking in ancient books and in long hours of quiet thought the secrets which lay beyond the life of man and all his knowledge. Hour after hour, day after day, month after month, he sat in meditation. His mind became quiet, almost as if it were empty of all thoughts and feelings; only he centred his thought as it were on a great question. Sometimes men would have said that he slept, for he hardly moved, hardly noticed anything around him and was as if far away in a kind of nothingness. He hardly ever remembered to eat and he grew thin and weak. No one now would have recognized the handsome Prince who had ridden out of his father's kingdom.

One day, as he sat in such deep and far-away thought, which was not really thinking at all, his overstrained body gave way and he sank senseless and fainting upon the ground. He lay as if he were dead, but a shepherd boy who came by, found him. The boy's first thought was to shelter the man from the hot sun, so he cut branches and built a bower to shade him and as he laid the branches near, flowers unfolded and fruit grew upon the branches and the boy knew that he must have found a god asleep. He brought up one of his goats and from its bag of milk he squeezed the teats so that a little milk ran into Siddartha's mouth. He was very careful, in trying to help, not to touch the Prince for in that country those of lowly birth were thought to be unclean and no one of a higher class or caste could let anyone so poor come near to him, even to perform a menial task.

With the sun shaded from his head and a little milk, Siddartha came to himself and he asked the boy for a little more milk. The boy was afraid to hand him the cup, lest this great one should be defiled, but Siddartha spoke gently to him and as he spoke he said what many men have slowly come to know to be true.

"All men," he said, "have the same red blood. Men have spoken about princes and kings having 'blue blood' but this is not true. All men when they cry have the same salt tears. A baby when he comes into the world, looks much the same as another. One cannot see if he is of princely blood or born of poor parents. Those who deserve our respect and our honour are those who act rightly and who are always kind; it is those who are evil and cruel who are the lowest of men."

So Siddartha showed again that he had come to teach men a better way of thinking, a better way of living. He took the cup of milk from the peasant boy and he gave him his blessing.

Another day there came past the place where Siddartha sat a great band of musicians and dancing girls. The musicians had drums to beat and fifes to play which made a sort of whistling tune and one of them had a stringed zither, from which he plucked sweet tuneful music. The girls as they went by also made a tinkling sound, for they had many bracelets on their arms and bangles also on their ankles. One of the girls was singing as she went to the accompaniment of the zither:

Fair goes the dancing, when the zither's tuned;
Tune for us the zither neither high nor low,
And we will dance away the hearts of men.
The string that is overstretched must break and the music
  dies,
The string that is overslack is dumb and music flies.
Tune for us the zither, neither low nor high.

The Prince listened and he did not frown as many holy men would have done because the pretty girl was like a butterfly, fluttering for just a short time in the sunshine. He listened to the words she sang and he wondered.

"There is wisdom in that little song," he said. "With all my sitting here and thinking and trying hard to understand about men and their lives, I am like an overstrung wire that gives out no music, when it is plucked. My strength is going from me and my thoughts cannot rise to heaven and I am doing nothing which is useful and good."

As Siddartha sat thinking such dejected thoughts, there came a graceful and very lovely young woman, dark-haired and wearing a crimson robe. She looked very much alive and well and happy. On one strong arm she carried her baby son and with the other she held upon her head a bowl of food. Now the place where Siddartha had chosen to sit was the ancient shrine of a wood god and the woman, who was called Sujata and who was the wife of Sinani the great landowner of the district, had come up to the shrine to bring a thank-offering to the wood god. Many months before she had come and had prayed there, telling the god how happy she was to be married and to be able to love and to serve a wonderful husband, but that they had not yet had a child, and she prayed earnestly that she might have a son and so complete her happiness. She had then brought gifts of food and flowers to the place and she had said that if she had a son, then she would bring a special bowl of food fit only for the gods.

So now Sujata came with her gift and found Siddartha seated beneath the sacred tree and, thinking that he must be the god himself, she offered him the milk curd that she had brought in a golden bowl and she anointed his hands with perfume. Siddartha ate the curd which was like a rich creamy cheese or thick yoghurt and suddenly he was filled with such youthful strength that it seemed like a miracle. So changed was he that Sujata indeed thought he was like a god. He asked her then what was the food she had brought and she told him how she had tried to make a perfect gift in return for the great joy she had in bearing a son.

She had taken a hundred of the finest cows of her husband's herd and with their milk she had fed fifty other cows that were white and fine and healthy and with their milk she had fed twenty-five others even finer and with their milk twelve others and with their milk the six best cows of all. So all the rich purity of the milk had been made better and better. Then she had heated the milk with fine spices and with rice which had been grown from carefully chosen seed set in new good ground and plucked grain by perfect grain.

Siddartha blessed the woman and blessed her baby and he talked a long time with her, while she told him of her simple life and how she loved her husband and her boy and was happy. There was nothing of evil in her heart. She had great love and perfect faith, as she had been taught. She

75

was like a lovely flower that grows in a quiet place and lives a life of beauty until it fades and dies. And Siddartha as his body had been strengthened by the milk food, also found his heart lifted to joy at such beauty and such simple goodness. It gave him hope that men could indeed live well and be happy.

When Sujata had gone away, Siddartha went in his new-found strength to a great tree which grew nearby. It was a banyan tree, a bodhi tree, which drops its longest branches on to the ground and the branches take root and grow so that a great bodhi tree is like a great outdoor cathedral with many columns and the leaves overall shade it like a vast tent. The time was near now for him to find the secret that he sought and the great tree in whose mighty shade he sat was long after to become a great and holy place visited by many pilgrims. And it is said that the tree is there still never having grown old or faded as even such big trees do after many years.

When Siddartha had been born, it had seemed as if the flowers in the garden, the dancing sunlight on the waters had shone brighter because of his birth, and when he rode out of his kingdom every sound in nature had been hushed to help him go unnoticed, and so now it seemed as if flowers and trees, animals and birds all around knew that a special time had come. Flowers sprang up where he walked, birds and small animals came close and no animal tried to hurt any other. Even the deadly poisonous snake swung from the tree without looking for its prey, butterflies and birds, squirrels and tiny monkeys all fluttered and skipped around as if showing him the best spot. And so Siddartha went on and sat down and night soon fell and all was quiet. This was to be the time of his great struggle and his deepest pain; this was a long dark night, but the last night before the dawn would come bringing a secret which would be like a light to shine for ever in the thoughts and the hearts of men, a light which would show to many men how they might find a way in the greatest darkness.

12. Siddartha Finds a way Through the Darkness

Night fell and Siddartha still sat beneath the great tree.

In the darkness all around there were many rustlings and small movements and most people would have been greatly afraid in that place for it was as if all the powers of darkness and evil, all the thoughts of hate and despair had come to prevent Siddartha from ever being able to help men as he longed to help them. Mara, the Prince of Darkness and of all evil powers, brought with him all the horrid thoughts that live because of man's ignorance and cruelty and all the glooms and fears gathered around. Sometimes they appeared as shadows; they muttered like far off thunder and when lightning flickered they looked like horrid beasts lurking in the darkness. Everything seemed to be trying to keep Siddartha in his new-found strength from thinking any holy and peaceful thoughts.

Then there came to Siddartha the ten GREAT SINS to

tempt him and to disturb his thoughts further. First came Attavanda, who always holds a mirror so that she can see only her own face and she is one who thinks only about herself. She whispered to the Prince that he must seek for the great truth, the deep secret of Life, for himself and then he would be the most powerful of gods. But Siddartha did not listen to her, knowing that he wanted the Truth for all men.

Then came Visikitcha who is also called Doubt and he

whispered that Siddartha was trying to find out something which no one could ever find. Men would never be different. Deep in his heart this Prince of men had to fight hard to overcome such thoughts, but he did win with Hope.

Then came False Faith, Sillabbat-paramasa, who defied any new hope and said there were enough priests and temples already and no one wanted another religion. But Siddartha thought that he was seeking a Faith, which would live more in men's hearts and minds than in any temples and church services.

Fourthly there came to him Passion, the King of the pleasure of love. He came carrying his bow with its arrows of great desire and with him came visions of beautiful faces and the sound of lovely voices, which sang of the love which men and women have for each other, that love which seems to most men the sweetest and most beautiful gift of all life, giving to man a godlike power and to woman the lovely gift of comfort. These surely were enough to set aside all pain and sorrow. The loveliest of the dancers in this company came close to Siddartha, hoping to make him forget his seeking and his own loneliness, urging him to remember only the warmth and the wonder of human love, and, when he still would not listen, the visions drew away and there came out of the darkness one who looked exactly like Yasodhara and she held out her arms to the Prince and wept and begged him to return to her and to remember the happiness and delight of their being together.

Siddartha said to her, "You are a deceitful shadow of the true Yasodhara and all that you say is also like a shadow, for there is a greater and more lasting love than that which men and women have for the beauty and the strength which fades and even for the deep affection which can also die."

As Siddartha refused the vision of his wife, a great cry

rang out and the beautiful company faded into smoke with many little flames that flickered in the outer darkness and then went out.

In the utter darkness then came six more terrible Sins, visions that were horrible and frightening. Fatigha or Hate came, wearing a girdle of serpents and as she cursed, the serpents hissed, but when Siddartha looked without fear there was silence again. Then came Ruparaga, who is greedy of time and snatches at each moment of pleasure as it passes, and Aruparaga, Fame, who tempts great heroes from self-love and the desire to be important, then Pride and Self Righteousness, Ignorance and Fear and Wrong. All these came up out of the darkness in a great storm. The earth shook and the heavens broke into drenching rain and everywhere the air was filled with horrid shapes and horrid sounds.

In the midst sat Siddartha, the Prince with the quiet heart, and even in the storm the leaves of the tree above him did not move except to shelter him better. So had passed the first and second watches of the night and in the third watch there was a stillness and then, in a great light, Siddartha saw how man had already travelled a long way from a more savage and more cruel past. Just as a climber might sit upon a high peak and look back all the long way he had come, noting the difficult and the dangerous places which he had passed by safely, so Siddartha saw the past lives of men. Each life was lived according to all the past lives and each man had the power to improve himself or to make the life in his place a little better and so when death came to him, all was a little better for the future.

Then in the next hour Siddartha, wholly absorbed in a wonder of thoughts, came to a closer understanding of man and of all the ages long gone by and of the time still to come while men lived on earth and his thought went out too from this small world into the Universe of greater space and he knew that in all space and in the timeless that the mind of man could not understand, there was a Power and a Purpose for life, which had planned for goodness and created beauty. Every little thing which was right and good worked for the plan and every little thing which was bad and wrong hindered it and made for longer suffering and misunderstanding.

In the fourth watch there came to Siddartha the secret of man's Sorrow, which is like his shadow and is a part of living. All the things, which a man tries to get to make him forget the things which frighten him, all the pleasures and ambitions, wealth, power, fame, conquest in battle, beautiful clothes, rich food and even love, all these he saw were like the drinking of salt water, the more one had the more one wanted and there was no satisfaction. Also the more one took for oneself, the more others must suffer, and so sorrow and pain could only increase. But if a man accepts his life and tries to live well he may in time find a heavenly peace, for although this is beyond all dreaming there is in everyone this hope, this overall, underall desire, to strive upwards towards goodness and peace.

Dawn came at last and Siddartha, now to be called the Buddha, which means the Enlightened One, had come from the darkness into the light. Now he would pass among men not as a Prince or a great King, but as one who carried with him a light of goodness and peace which would shed itself all around him, for he had come to a greater understanding of things than any man had ever come before. Now he would go back to the world of men and try to teach men to understand a little more of the purpose of living, to understand a little more of the Power which men had called "God".

Morning came and the sun rose and nature in all her loveliness filled the place with colour and light and song and they said that for miles around men rose with a new sense of life. Robbers gave back their plunder, kings at war made peace, many who were sick became well and those who had to die fell into their last sleep smiling with joy. It is said that this wonderful feeling came even to Yasodhara far away, sitting upon her bed sadly thinking of her lost husband. Everywhere people gathered in the streets and looked out across the fields to see this wondrous morning and the beasts and birds of prey lay down with the other creatures and did them no harm.

And the Buddha walked out from beneath his great tree and looked towards the rising sun and sang a great song, for the old life had gone for ever and a new life could now begin.

13. The Buddha Returns Home

Back in the land of the Sakya people, the King Suddhodana was growing old. Yasodhara still mourned for Siddartha and could never be comforted, though she had joy in her little son. From every traveller who came, she and the King sought for news of the lost Prince, but no one seemed to have heard of him.

For the seventh year since the morning of their sad awakening, spring came again with light and beauty and the scent of blossom, and one day Yasodhara sat in the palace gardens watching her little son at play. She was no longer beautiful, for she had grown older and grief had made her pale and thin. She no longer wore beautiful colours, but dressed in the plain coarse white robe which widows wore in that country and a fold of the robe she held to cover her hair. She walked slowly and listlessly. Her once lovely eyes were dark and sad and often dimmed with tears.

Rahula, her son, now nearly seven years old, was running

amid the fountains and feeding the coloured fish in the pools. His mother sat and watched him and looked up also to see the birds flying over the gardens, moving in flocks as they always did at that time of year. Then because they could fly away and she could not, her thoughts went out as ever to her love for whom she still longed all the time.

Then there came running to her some ladies of the court, who said, "Princess, there is a great caravan of merchants even now coming through the south gate of the city. They have travelled to many far-away lands, far away even to the sea, and they have the most wonderful treasures for sale, brass bowls and carved ivory, great swords of steel and lovely cloth all embroidered with gold."

Yasodhara hardly seemed to hear, but then one girl said quietly, "Princess, they also bring news of the Lord Siddartha. They say they have seen him and heard him. They say he has become a great Teacher and that everywhere he goes men love and follow him. They say, too, that he is coming back to his home."

Yasodhara's heart was overfilled with joy and a great thankfulness for the end of the long, sad waiting. She had the merchants brought to the palace and sent word to the King. The merchants answered her questions in words which seemed puzzling:

"Yes, we have seen the Prince and he is now the Prince of all and the Friend of all. He is on his way here and he will be here before the summer rains. We have heard his teaching and we have seen how, as he goes from place to place, men everywhere try to follow him in love and those who listen to him seek to live a better life."

The merchants told Yasodhara what they had heard men say about a certain night when all the powers of darkness seemed to ride abroad and how afterwards there had been the most wonderful morning. First then he had gone to the holy city of Benares and after a little he had chosen five disciples whom he had taught. Yasad, the great Prince of that land, had come with fifty-four of his nobles and all had then gone out as holy men teaching a new doctrine. The Buddha, the Enlightened One, as they now called him, had then gone back to Bimbisara's kingdom as he had made a promise to the King. He had taught the people there and was now coming home.

Yasodhara rewarded the merchants and asked them by which road they thought the Prince would come and how far away he was, and they said he was still about a month's journey away. The King then sent out swift messengers to take loving greetings to his son and to make urgent prayers that he should come with all haste. The messengers went off one after the other as the King grew more and more impatient, but when each came to where the Buddha was they found him always surrounded by crowds of people, and when they sat down to listen to him, they quite forgot their messages. Thoughts of the tired old King and the waiting princess quite faded from their minds and they could only join in and listen.

At last the King sent Udayi, a chief man of his court and told him to stop his ears with cotton waste, so that he could get right up to the Prince and give his message. And when he had the message, the Buddha set out straightway for his home, and the news of his coming came before him and great preparations were made to welcome him as the King's Son.

Near the south gate of the city they erected a bright pavilion, its walls of silk, gold embroidered and all its poles and pillars wreathed in flowers. All the flags went up and the roads were strewn with the sweet branches of palm.

Great elephants were richly caparisoned and all the dancing girls assembled and prepared with music and flowers for a great festival of welcome. Far out on the road men were posted to give news of their Prince's coming; as soon as they saw him they would come running.

Yasodhara, eager to be the first to greet her lord, rode out in her litter to the city gate and sat there watching the many people who gathered there. Everyone was watching and waiting, expecting the swift messengers and expecting then to see their Prince come riding on a great horse.

Then almost unnoticed in the crowd there came a holy man clad in the yellow robe that such men wear in that country. He carried the usual begging bowl and as he came he begged for alms. Two others followed him. Yet he who walked first was so gentle and yet so stately that as he came men, women and children did notice him and some ran to bring gifts for his bowl and others followed him asking each other who this wonderful priest might be. The odd procession, so different from what they expected, came up to the gate and suddenly then Yasodhara came forward from her litter and cried out that this was the Prince Siddartha and she fell at his feet and wept.

Back at the Palace, sitting in state on his throne, King Suddhodana was furious when he heard that his son had come in this fashion, dressed and behaving like a beggar and taking food even from the poorest people. His love and his longing for his son were quite swallowed up in his anger and he called for his horse and rode through the streets, without any escort, scattering the people from his path and riding furiously. He came to the gate and he saw his son with the great crowds all around and as the Buddha's eyes met his, his anger went away and he dismounted and came and knelt before his son. In that moment he knew that the

Prince, for all his humble dress and his beggar's bowl, had yet a great and holy strength mightier than that of any King upon a throne. Yet quietly he reproached his son for staying away so long and that he should now return to his kingdom and to his wife in such a state of poverty and the Buddha replied, "But it is the custom of my race." This the King could not understand for all his family and his ancestors had been mighty and powerful kings and great warriors, but the Buddha explained that he was not thinking of his kingly ancestors, but of those who in the past had been teachers of men and who had lived in poverty and walked and talked with the common people.

Then the Buddha said that he had come back to those who loved him because he had a great debt to pay and he had brought with him a great treasure. At the word "treasure" the King's heart leapt with joy and he enquired where the treasure was. Then the Buddha took his father's hand and Yasodhara walked on his other side and they passed through the streets and through the throngs of people. The great King and his son the Prince and the lovely Princess who had never been seen to walk in the streets of the city went along listening to the Buddha, so enrapt that they did not even notice their new humility. Yasodhara seemed to have regained her youth and loveliness and hardly anyone noticed that as they reached the palace, the King himself was carrying in his hands the beggar's bowl.

14. *The Buddha Teachs his People*

The great Prince Siddartha had returned to his father's city and to the great kingdom, which men had expected him to rule. He came now to the King's magnificent palace and he sat in the great audience room. His lovely wife Yasodhara sat at his feet and the little prince, Rahula, stood close at his side. The King was there too and for the first time, as he sat in his court, no eye looked towards *him*, yet from the day so many years before when he had become King, he had never known a single moment when every man near him had not looked towards him, waiting for him to speak, waiting for him to say something which would affect all their lives, waiting for him to pronounce a judgment which meant that they must die. Now all were assembled and all the great lords and the priests and the wise men and everyone looked only at the Buddha.

He spoke to them and for many hours, many days, he taught them. Only a little can be told of his teaching and of his great wisdom. It takes too long to tell and it is not easy to understand.

He taught that men's lives are like little drops of water that flow together to make a stream and a river and that as, in the end, a river reaches the sea, so there is an ocean of all life. From the ocean the tiny droplets are caught up into the skies, becoming for a time invisible in the air and skies, but soon they return again as rain upon the hills and so flow towards the sea again. So life goes on and goes round and round. In some mysterious fashion a man is bound up with lives in time past and equally his life affects the lives in time future. Within each single life a man can, if he reaches out to understand the secret of life, make all life better for all men for he will become kind and gentle and good and each single life which is made better makes the whole world better.

He taught that far beyond man's sight and beyond man's ordinary understanding was a great creative Power, which made the universe and ordered all for good. Everywhere that we might look, we see this life power having a pattern of beauty. But man was very small and very stupid and he could not yet see the pattern of the whole.

When man did well and acted with gentleness and kindness to others he helped to make the whole pattern right and when he was cruel and evil he made a mistake and this had to be somehow put right. Men were often sad because they wanted the wrong things, but if they could find the right way then they would be truly happy. It was not easy for a man to follow the right way, but there were some general rules for men to follow which would bring them in the right direction.

The Buddha gave the following rules :

Do not kill.
Give and take, but never take by force or by fraud.
Do not lie or bear false witness.
Do not weaken the body with drugs or strong drink.
Do not take your neighbour's wife.

He said too that it was much more important to behave properly to other people than to pray often to the unseen powers. Each man and woman, said the Buddha, is, in his innermost heart, alone and each one is often bewildered and even afraid, but if he can make a right and loving relationship with other human beings and if he will reach out to understand and to respect both the natural powers and the supernatural powers, then it will be as if strong arms were always around him and he will have no need for fear at any time.

Each man and each woman is like the centre of a compass, which on earth shows us the north and the south, the east and the west, but there is also the sky above and the ground below and this makes six different directions. We may think about these six points in the way shown in the picture on the next page, directing towards them our thoughts and our love.

For forty-five more years, after he returned to the Sakya Kingdom, the Buddha taught the people, sometimes making journeys to other places, and his followers went throughout all India and travelled far across the seas and the mountains and deserts but all towards the east. Buddhists never came to the western lands, where the sun goes down into the sea, but the great Greek King Alexander came to N.W. India and his army returned from there and some of the things

ABOVE–What men have called GOD–that which you cannot see, but you can study what other men have learned and said.

NORTH–Close friends and loved relations who help to keep you from loneliness and sorrow.

EAST–Parents and those who care for you when you are young.

WEST–Husband or wife and children who care for you when you are older.

SOUTH–Teachers who have for you many rich gifts.

BELOW–NATURE–all the other things on earth which you may see and learn about and care for.

we find today in both India and the Mediterranean lands show that soldiers and merchants met and talked together in the ancient days.

Before he died the Buddha foretold that five hundred years later there would be born on earth another Buddha, another Enlightened One, and men would call him the Teacher of Brotherly Love and he would be the Christ and Saviour of the western peoples. And so it was, for Jesus was born five hundred years afterwards and he became the great teacher for men in the western world, Europe and Britain and America.

Only in the last hundred years or so have men learned to make machines which travel fast on the land, ships which go strongly and quickly across the oceans and planes that fly even more quickly through the air. Now the peoples of the western lands and the peoples of the eastern lands can meet often, but they do not always understand each other. Even the words "West" and "East" are not quite right, for the world is round and "the West" is east of "the East" and most of "the East" lies westwards from America.

Many people in India forgot the Buddha's teaching and kept an older religion, but in this too the wisest men can see what is true and what is good. The Europeans went to India to conquer and because they did not understand they thought the Indian people were all ignorant and heathen, but in every land some men have learned from other men what is the best way to live and how goodness and kindness may be increased. To be strong and powerful may seem to be good, but one can use strength for evil too. The greatest of men, those teachers who seemed to be greater than other men, have always taught men to be kind and gentle and considerate of others.

94